AF413200

ISBN : 979-8-9898745-2-1

For permissions requests, contact:

Ervin & Holland Publication
73-730 Hwy 111 Ste 4
Palm Desert CA 9220

DEDICATED TO
MY FAMILY

Do you know what equality, equity, diversity, and inclusion mean?

They might seem like big words, but they're really as simple as 1,2,3....

Equity

is like stacking the boxes on top of each other but only placing them when needed to give everyone the same height.

Where should I put the boxes to make everyone equal?

E
Q
U
I
T
Y

EQUITY
eq·ui·ty
the quality of being
fair and open-minded.

Diversity

is like having a box of crayons and every color inside the box is different.

Could you imagine the crayon box full of the same colors and never being able to see something different?

CRAYONS
Grey
CRAYONS
Blue
Yellow

Diversity

di·ver·si·ty

the state of being diverse; variety.

Justice is JUST US.
With love and respect
for each other we can
do anything together.

JUSTICE

jus·tice
a concern for
justice, peace, and
genuine respect for
people.

Inclusion
is like seeing a new kid on the playground alone. Go ask if they are okay with making a new friend.

Inclusion

in·clu·sion

the action or state of including or of being included within a group or structure.

EQUALITY
looks like every child is getting a chance to be great no matter the color of their skin or gender.

Equality

e·qual·i·ty

the state of being equal, in status, rights, and opportunities.

Empathy

is like when your friend
is sad because they
don't have lunch and
you decide to share
your favorite sandwich
with them.

Empathy
em·pa·thy
the ability to understand and share
the feelings of another.

Compassion
is like asking a friend who uses a
wheelchair if they want help up
the hill to the playground.

Compassion
com·pas·sion
Worried and concerned for the sufferings of others.

2024
get
well

This book was made to give children a simple understanding of what all these wonderful words mean. If we decide to love and respect one another our world will become a great place to live in.

Equity, Diversity, Equality, and Inclusion for Kids it's as simple as 1,2,3...